Pen&Ink
Techniques

Pen&Ink Techniques

Frank Lohan

Contemporary Books, Inc.
Chicago

Library of Congress Cataloging in Publication Data

Lohan, Frank J
  Pen and ink techniques.

  Includes index.
  1. Pen drawing—Technique.   I. Title.
NC905.L6   741.2′6   78-57478
ISBN 0-8092-7439-6
ISBN 0-8092-7438-8 pbk.

Published by Contemporary Books, Inc.
180 North Michigan Avenue, Chicago, Illinois 60601
Manufactured in the United States of America
Library of Congress Catalog Card Number: 78-57478
International Standard Book Number: 0-8092-7439-6 (cloth)
                                    0-8092-7438-8 (paper)

Published simultaneously in Canada by
Beaverbooks, Ltd.
150 Lesmill Road
Don Mills, Ontario M3B 2T5
Canada

This book is dedicated to the hundreds of students whose years of interest and enthusiasm for this rewarding medium have given me both opportunity and incentive for continuing my own study and development with the pen.

Contents

Introduction

Each art form developed certain conventions as it evolved through the centuries. Sculpture deals with form, surface, and dimension but generally ignores color—except for the long-forgotten cigar store Indian. Painting deals with color and generally ignores both line and a third dimension in the finished product. Pen and ink sketching has neither dimension nor color to assist in creating a visual illusion—just lines, dots, and black areas on white paper.

These conventions—restrictions—still allow for a vast amount of individuality of style, approach, and interpretation in each of these mediums. Each individual's technique is as personal and distinctive as his or her handwriting. Your technique, your style, that distinctive way *you* have of making and arranging the lines, dots, and dark areas to create your own statement on the paper will evolve if you really have the desire and if you persevere. It will by and large give your

sketches that uniquely personal quality that will be recognizable as yours even before the viewer sees your name on a work. This does not happen immediately. First you must train your hand, wrist, and arm to the pen; you must learn and practice the fundamentals; you must make mistakes and learn from them. As an important part of your practice you must—heresy of heresies to some purists!—copy the work or portions thereof of other accomplished line artists to learn just how they created their particular effects. All the practice work you can manage becomes your inventory of ingredients from which you select those you need to create your own original works.

This book evolved from several years of teaching pen and ink sketching in adult education facilities. It was developed to meet several needs, those of the artist accomplished in some other medium as well as those of the artistically inclined person who has done little more than write his name with a pen. Persons at all levels of achievement can experience that particular gratification that comes with creation of a unique and personal artistic expression with pen and ink. I have seen it happen at all levels of achievement in my classes and have enjoyed each such creation just as much as the student did.

Next to pencil sketching, pen and ink is the cleanest, simplest, least expensive medium to work in. At the minimum, an artist's fountain pen and some unlined index cards can be taken in a pocket virtually anywhere and used with no elaborate preparation or set up required. Some of my students carry them on vacations, on business trips, and even to the doctor's or dentist's office and use them to good purpose.

Pen and ink line work is especially suitable for printing inexpensively. You can make your very own note paper, greeting cards, and even limited-edition reproductions for very little more than the cost of having typewritten material printed. See Part III for some ideas on how to lay out what you want printed.

Pen and ink is a totally absorbing medium for those who become serious about it. It can be excellent therapy for anyone whose mobility is limited and who has time hanging heavy on his hands. Hours can literally seem like minutes when working on a sketch. This last statement may seem trite, but only those who have done some sketching with the pen know how long even an apparently simple sketch takes to execute effectively.

This book is divided into four sections. Any of the four can be approached as your needs and level of accomplishment dictate. There is, however, a good bit of logic for the beginner to start at the beginning and seriously practice the hand and wrist training the various suggested practice exercises will help to develop. Before you can sketch really well you must know your tools, not just the types of paper and pens, but also the kinds of

marks you will make on the paper. Dexterity and control in making the marks is all important to successful sketching. When you want to cover an area with hatch marks to produce a gray tone, you must be able to make uniform marks to avoid a patchy, unorganized effect on the paper. To do this will require some diligent practice until you can make uniformly spaced hatch marks of uniform line weight when you need them. Similar control will be required for graded tone effects. This control will only be achieved by practice and more practice.

Part I: Basics, covers some of the things you should know about the tools and materials you will be working with. It shows the simple grid system for copying, enlarging, and reducing a sketch. It contains some guidelines for making your sketches the proper size for inexpensive matting and framing in standard-size frames. So many students are so eager to get sketching that they ignore these considerations until the sketch is completed. Then, if they want to frame their work, they find they must trim it or go to expensive custom framing. So my advice is to plan ahead by reading the Matting portion of Part I before you start a sketch. This section also contains some suggested practice strokes. These are by no means all of the strokes you will need, but reasonable control of the suggested ones will go a long way toward building up that inventory you will need for successful sketching.

Part II: Beginning, includes eleven different subjects. These subjects are not examples of great art. They are simply intended to be exercises crammed with as many problems of texture, light, and shade as possible to offer you as much practice in one exercise as possible. Almost all are greatly overworked sketches and this was intentional. Outline drawings are included for each of these eleven sketches to make it easier for the novice to get his working pencil sketch properly and completely done prior to starting the ink work. In all cases a good, complete pencil sketch is essential first when sketching. Problems of proper size and perspective will not magically solve themselves as you put the ink on the paper if they have not been correctly solved beforehand with the pencil. When the sketch is complete, the pencil lines are erased with a soft eraser such as Artgum. These eleven sketches build one on the other as they introduce various texturing techniques. Portions of this section will prove to be good practice even for the intermediate or advanced student, as will the copying of portions of the work of any good line artist you may come across.

Part III: Intermediate, contains a number of specific subjects with far fewer direct how-to steps than in Part I. The subject matter is more artistic, less overworked than the beginners' exercises. Using the texturing techniques developed in Part I, we here apply them to subjects that are more likely to be like those you will want to sketch for yourself. That very interesting material, scratchboard, is introduced in this section also, with two different ways of using it. Once you get involved with ink you will almost certainly want to make your own greeting cards and/or notepaper. Some suggestions begin in this section.

Part IV: Reference, contains a wide variety of different types of sketches with virtually no how-to instructions. It is meant to be a source of ways to proceed when you are sketching on your own and want to see how to produce various effects. This section may be of help in at least showing you a way to go; certainly it does not pretend to show *the* way to sketch everything. It gives a few hints on making foregrounds interesting, especially in landscapes. Many structural materials such as bricks, stone, siding, stucco, shingles, and wood are shown, as well as the treatment of rocks both in the foreground and in the background. An attempt was made to include as many different subjects in this section as seems practical. It ends up with examples of the use of different inking tools such as the brush, palette knife, and even twigs.

Your own imagination is the only limit to the things you can create with this wonderfully simple and direct art medium. It is my hope that this book, as limited as it may be, will serve to awaken in you some of the enthusiasm that I have for the pen and that I have seen come to light in many of my students through the past few years.

Pen&Ink Techniques

Part I: Basics

Some knowledge of the tools and materials used in pen and ink work is essential. Frequently at the start of a session of my classes some students show up all set to work in ink, but they have a commercial pad of paper that was made for charcoal sketching. Or, worse yet, they have a pad of newsprint. These papers were manufactured for other purposes than ink. They therefore create some problems the beginner can well do without.

This section starts with a discussion of some of the kinds of paper that are suitable for pen and ink work. The usual smooth, hard-surfaced bristol board remains perhaps the most widely used paper for this kind of work. It is not, however, the only paper quite suited for ink. A rough watercolor paper, with the broken-line effect that it frequently causes, can bring an interesting softness to an ink sketch. Read the suggestions, but also experiment for yourself.

Pens, as noted in this section, come in many styles. The simplest is the nib pen; the most expensive are the technical pens. Most artist supply stores carry several makes of each kind of pen and will gladly show you the features offered by each make. How much you spend for a pen will be determined by how serious you are about sketching. If you really intend to get into it, then the more expensive artist's fountain pen with a couple of points will last a lifetime—and will free you from carrying around ink bottles.

The easiest way to copy, enlarge, or reduce a sketch or a picture that you want to sketch is with the grid system shown in this section. For those whose drawing skills are not well-developed, this scheme is essential to avoid gross errors in perspective. If you do not want to put lines directly on the subject picture, you can create a grid on tracing paper and lay it over your subject. Then put the working grid on your sketch paper, and you are ready to go.

It is recommended that you take to heart the comments about minimizing outlines. This will be the biggest single step you can initially take to make your sketches look really professional and to get away from that coloring-book appearance in your work.

Paper

Paper is no problem for pen and ink work. For practice, almost any good typing paper will do. For final sketches, however, a heavier paper is better.

One of the best papers is *bristol board*. This comes in several weights—two-ply, three-ply, and up. It is a hard-surfaced paper and takes ink very well. It comes in pads of various sizes—9 × 12, 11 × 14, and so on.

Watercolor paper is also interesting because of its texture. This texture can lend real interest to a pen sketch. Some watercolor papers such as Morilla board come in an off-white or beige color that looks quite good with a dark brown ink.

Watercolor papers come in different weights—80 pound, 140 pound, etc. They are available in pads of various sizes, also.

Sketches can also be done on clear *acetate film*. Make your pencil composition and lay a piece of acetate over it. Use drawing ink that says "for film" on the box for best results.

You can make a simple watercolor underlay for an acetate sketch. The sketch has all the detail line work, and the simple swatches of color under it can give you a really bright, snappy result. The color should be on a separate sheet of paper under the acetate film.

Acetate Film

Tracing vellum is useful to place over your sketch to try different ways of creating a difficult texture. You can try several ways of doing it before you commit yourself to putting ink on your final drawing.

Vellum looks white but is nearly transparent when placed over a pencil drawing. You can also make a watercolor underlay for a vellum sketch, just as with the acetate film, for a different effect.

Any surface that takes ink well can be used for sketching. *Colored papers* or *mat board* also give interesting effects.

Scratchboard, a special paper, is discussed and demonstrated later in this book.

Pens

There are several types of pens for sketching. At the right the standard *nib* pen is shown. This is the least expensive, the holder costing about 25 cents and each point about 20 cents. There are many different points available in varying degrees of flexibility.

The best to start with is the Crowquill point.

The nib-type pen can be used with any kind of india ink, but it must be kept clean by frequent wiping while you are using it.

The *technical pen*, often called the *Rapidograph* type, is shown at the right. This is a tubular point pen; it has no flexibility, and each point makes just one line width. The 000 or 3×0 is good to start with.

The big advantage of this type is that it is a fountain pen and eliminates both carrying ink and constant dipping.

Many different points are available for different line widths.

NEVER use ordinary india ink in these pens. Special ink is required.

There are several makes of technical pens available. They cost about $7 to $10.

The *artist's fountain pen* shown at the right is also conveniently portable and has several different, interchangeable points available. There are several different makes available, some of which have lettering points as well as sketching points.

NEVER use ordinary india ink in these pens, either. Special ink is available for them.

The fountain pens have flexible points, allowing different line widths without changing the point.

They cost about $7 to $12.

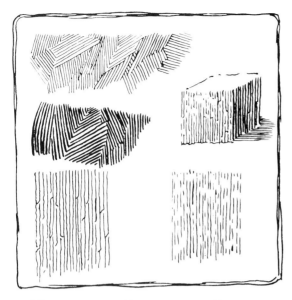

Avoid this—uneven tone.

Some Basic Guidelines

In most sketches with pen and ink, tone (shading) is created with groups of parallel lines called *hatching*.

To be effective hatching must be uniform—the lines must be evenly spaced and of equal weight.

Practice groups of hatching as at the left until you can do it uniformly.

To create darker tones sometimes use thicker lines when hatching and sometimes use *cross-hatching* by hatching over in a different direction.

Some practice suggestions are shown at the left—along with the kind of effect you should avoid.

Stippling (dots) is often useful. First make a uniform tone as in A; then dot over to darken as in B.

Grass strokes, foliage, and tree trunks should also be practiced until you can get the effect you want easily and quickly.

Practice Strokes

Some of the pen strokes you will need are illustrated here. Practice is essential to developing any skill, and it takes a certain amount of skill to get reasonably uniform hatching, cross-hatching, and graded tones when you need them for your sketching.

These are by no means all of the strokes you will need, but practicing the strokes below will help in gaining some of the pen control you should have to do a credible job of sketching.

Hatching

Cross-hatching

Hatching

Broken hatching

Graded tone

Graded tone

Graded tone

Graded tones

Foreground trees

Grass strokes

Background trees

Stippling

Drawn with
Hunt #104 pen.

Pen Size

Suit the pen to the size and character of the sketch.

Too fine a point can give a washed-out appearance to the sketch; too coarse can detract from the delicate details.

Drawn with
Hunt #100 pen.

Drawn with
fountain pen.

A heavy fountain pen can be quite effective, as you will see later. However, for the sketch at the right it was much too coarse.

Copying Pictures

Use the grid system. Draw squares over the picture; then draw the same number of squares across and down on your paper. If you want to enlarge the picture, you will have larger squares on the paper. To reduce it your squares will be smaller. To make it the same size your squares will be the same size.

Then draw the picture, using the grid of squares as a guide. If you draw the squares lightly in pencil, you can do it directly on the sheet for your final ink sketch. Draw lightly, as these lines must be erased when your sketch is completed.

An alternative method is to draw the squares and your full-size sketch on a piece of typewriter paper; then on the back of this sheet rub the side of your pencil lead where the lines are. Then place the sheet over your final sheet and draw over the sketch lines. The carbon from the pencil will leave an impression on the final sheet that you can ink over and easily erase when the sketch is completed. This minimizes the erasing you must do on your final drawing. Use a soft eraser like an Art Gum.

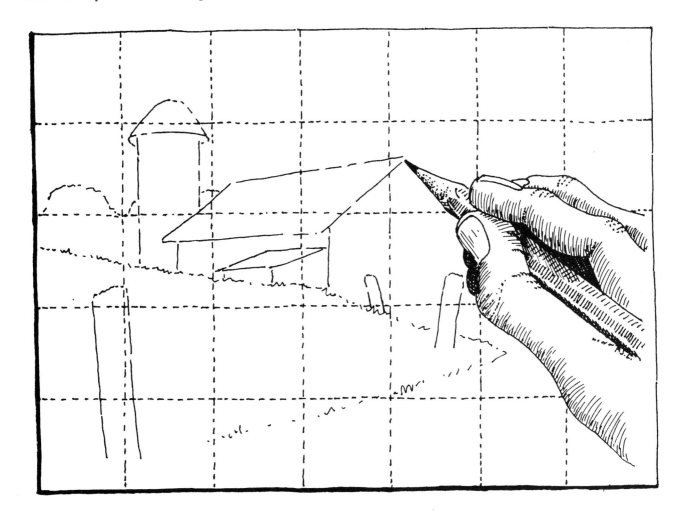

Easy Matting

Pen and ink sketches generally look best matted and hung in a simple frame. If you plan to frame your sketch, plan ahead for the frame and mat size you want.

Ready-made frames come in standard sizes and are less costly than custom frames. Some of the standard sizes as well as the suggested mat dimensions are shown below.

Mark your paper with pencil lines and keep your sketch within them.

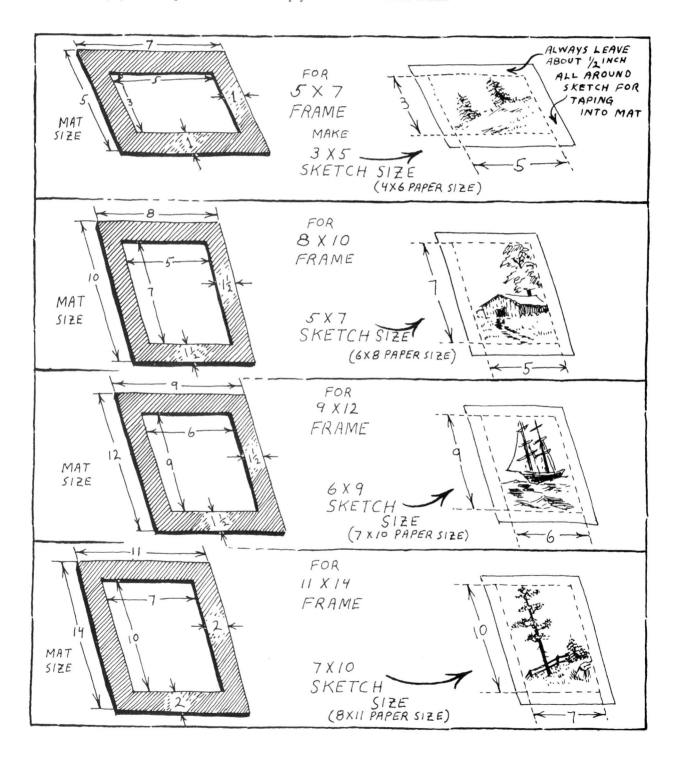

Minimizing Outlines

Make a pencil sketch. Then ink a few details in the sun and a few more in the shade.

Then use hatching and cross-hatching to create tones and shade.

If you outline everything first . . .

even when you shade it and tone it, your sketch will resemble a picture from a child's coloring book.

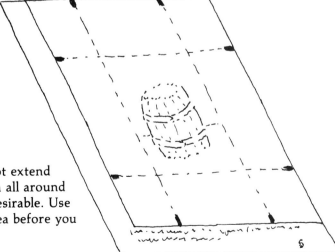

Pen and ink sketches look best when they do not extend under the mat when framed. A clean white area all around the sketch between the mat and the sketch is desirable. Use light pencil guidelines to frame in the sketch area before you start to ink, then erase them when finished.

NO OUTLINES

In a toned sketch, keep outlining to an absolute minimum. Let the toned areas themselves define the shapes.

Utilizing the dark-against-light and light-against-dark principle allowed practically no outlining in the upper sketch on this page and none at all in the lower sketch.

Part II: Beginning

The only effects you have at your disposal to create the illusion of depth, form, texture, and dimension with ink are light and dark tones. The most difficult thing for beginners to appreciate is that to show one thing in front of another requires that one of these things be lighter than the other or else they will blend together and become indistinct. When sketching from nature or from photographs, the artist must often force tones and shadows to serve his purpose, regardless of how they appear to the eye.

This section builds an inventory of strokes and approaches to this basic light-on-dark and dark-on-light principle. Starting with a simple barrel in which you see how to create the texture of old wood with short strokes and little dots and stabs of the pen, you still require careful light/dark juxtaposition in the upper left corner for definition of the subject. Be on the lookout in each of the eleven sketches

for this light/dark principle; it is one of the most important lessons you should learn from this section.

There is a brief mention for each of the eleven sketches as to what the purpose of the particular sketch is and what you should particularly look for and remember from the exercise.

Each exercise has a blank outline drawing preceding it. This is to be copied or traced and then completed, following the instructions on the page following the blank outline. If you make your sketch the same size as the illustration, it should be suitable for framing in an 8- by 10-inch frame with a mat opening of 5 by 7 inches.

An important part of any learning process is making mistakes. They teach us more than dozens of successes do. In the beginning phases of your work with the pen there will be drops of ink that mysteriously appear on your sketch or errors you would like to eliminate. Take heart, because there is a way that often can save your early sketches when this happens. A little patch cut from the white self-stick labels sold in all office supply stores can be placed over the blot or error. If this is in a busy area so that you can reconstruct the line work over the patch and cover all edges with line, it will become quite invisible, even to you when you know where it is.

Old Barrel—Outline and Instructions

This first lesson shows how to create the texture of an old, beat-up barrel. It also shows how to create roundness in a subject by the use of a shadow that gradually tapers into the light area. Note that in the brightest area almost no detail shows. The absence of detail indicates glare.

Whenever you have horizontal surfaces such as ground, roadways, paths, etc. in your sketch you must show such surfaces by the use of predominantly horizontal lines. If you use lines at other angles your surface will appear to tilt.

Copy or trace the outline of the barrel from this page and then proceed following the steps shown on the next page.

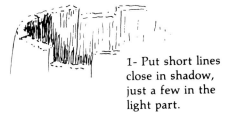

1- Put short lines
close in shadow,
just a few in the
light part.

2- Add more lines in
dark shadow. Emphasize
space between staves.

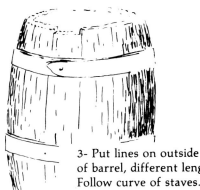

3- Put lines on outside
of barrel, different lengths.
Follow curve of staves. Draw
very few in highlight area.

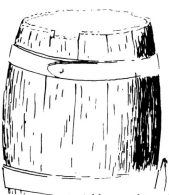

4- Add more lines in shadow
at right to deepen it.

5- Connect a few of
the vertical lines on
the staves with short
horizontal strokes.

6- Emphasize some of the
spaces between the staves.

7- Put some dots and
small squiggles all
over the barrel to
give a weathered
look to the wood.

8- Shade the hoops with
short, straight lines.
Put none in the highlight
areas.

9- Finish the rope with
short lines and dots.
Finish the shadow of
the barrel—use
horizontal lines.

10- Put pebbles and their
shadows on the ground.
Add other lines and squiggles.
Do not put too much on
the ground or it will be
too dark.

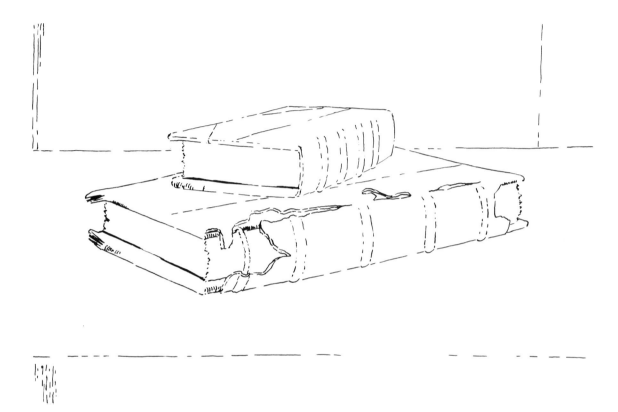

Old Books—Outline and Instructions

The Old Books introduces a background element that will be very important in many of your sketches. This is a more or less uniform tone. In this exercise the tone is broken up to provide a little more interest than a solid tone would.

It is important to note that each line in the background, from top to bottom, was made as one line. That is the pen was moved from top to bottom as if making one continuous line but was lifted to create the skips. Do not make the mistake of thinking that the discontinuous lines were placed on the paper at random. Note also that the space between the lines is less at the center of the sketch than it is at the edges. This provides a graduated tone which is a little lighter behind the dark books than it is at the edges of the sketch. Try to make this background as carefully as you can and keep the lines the same weight.

The basic strokes to produce the texture on the books were previously used to texture the barrel.

Remember to keep the strokes on the tablecloth horizontal.

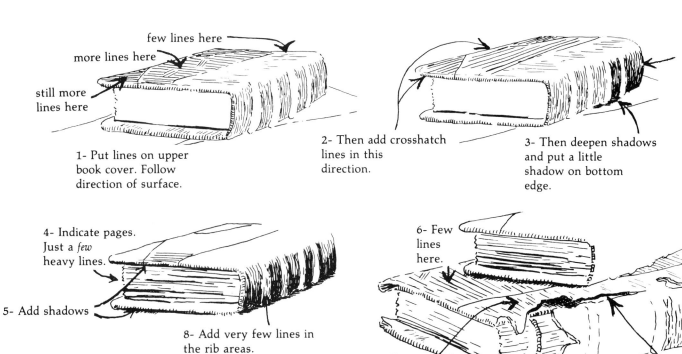

few lines here

more lines here

still more lines here

1- Put lines on upper book cover. Follow direction of surface.

2- Then add crosshatch lines in this direction.

3- Then deepen shadows and put a little shadow on bottom edge.

4- Indicate pages. Just a *few* heavy lines.

5- Add shadows

8- Add very few lines in the rib areas.

9- Do the background and tablecloth.

10- Touch up the dark areas if they need it.

6- Few lines here.

Fewer still here

7- Make broken edges of binding dark. Crosshatch the under layer. Then do the back of lower book.

Landscape

Trees and foliage must be kept light and airy to be effective in pen and ink sketches. It works out best if you put foliage masses in place first and then do the tree trunk or whatever is adjacent to the foliage.

Remember that the bottom and the side of foliage that is away from the sun should be shaded; the side toward the sun should have no great amount of detail. This enhances the idea of glare from the sun on these surfaces.

Practice the following exercises before going on to the next sketches.

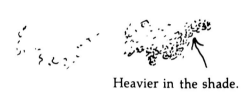

Heavier in the shade.

First like this . . .

. . . then deepen the shadows.

Another way: crosshatch to make the shadows.

First put the leaf masses in; then finish the tree trunk.

Do not draw all the bricks in a wall or building of brick. Some are not shown at all, some are shown by just two lines on the shaded side or just in outline, some are hatched a medium tone, and a few are darkened. Generally, in the shadow all the bricks are shown with a medium tone as the whole shade area is hatched over later.

First indicate the bricks you want to show.

Then darken those in the shade and a *few* in the sun.

Then finish shading and shadows.

Remember that you must show something dark against a light area and something light against a dark area.

Practice the little fence drawing, as you will do this very thing in the next sketch.

Brick Wall and Fence—Outline and Instructions

Here you are introduced to a few new textures . . . the foliage, the bricks, the grass.

The background is similar to the previous one but in this case it is plainer. All we want to do here is indicate with virtually no detail that there is a background line of trees present. Any detail work in these trees would only serve to confuse and blend with the details in the foreground.

Remember when showing distant things that detail should decrease with distance to achieve the aerial perspective that making things subdued and bluer does in painting.

Dark must show on light and light must show on dark. The iron fence in this exercise is partly against a light background and partly against a dark background. Note that the fence takes on the opposite tone from its background. Otherwise it would disappear.

Remember not to draw all the bricks in the wall. Also, do not put too much texture in the sidewalk or you will not be able to distinguish it from the grassy areas.

Where you show shadow, make it a uniform shadow. Do not just make patchy darker groups of lines with big light spaces between them. Make your shadows uniformly gray in tone with evenly spaced lines.

Start house this way.

Then add a few shingles on roof. Add more texture lines on side of house.

Then crosshatch window and shadow under eaves.

Put light foliage in first. Then darken right side of fence risers and bottom of stringers.

Then put in dark foliage and shadow under cap on brick wall.

Show bricks in shadow like this.

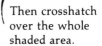

Then crosshatch over the whole shaded area.

Shadow on grass.

For shadow on sidewalk and street use horizontal strokes.

Sunlight on grass.

Follow surfaces of curb with texture lines.

Landscape—Outline and Instructions

This little landscape is primarily an exercise in light against dark and dark against light principles. The background tree line is a medium tone. Against this medium tone the lighter tree foliage must show and the darker evergreen trees and dark pickets must also show. In a case like this, do the background trees first. Then you can tell how dark and how light to make the superimposed details so that they do not become lost.

Remember to keep the bulk of your strokes in the roadway horizontal. Do not put any strokes in the roadway where it goes from right to left in the background. Just let the little dots which show the grass on either side define it.

First complete the background trees, shrubs, and the two evergreens. Then do the fence. Be sure to leave the light areas between the dark pickets and to darken between the light pickets.

Now you can tell just how much stippling to put into the foliage masses. Too much and they will disappear into the background.

Where branches cross the dark parts of the trees, be sure to leave white above them.

Where the path curves away in the background, do not put any texture lines at all in the path. Make the grass strokes on each side of the path a little denser. This will define the path in this area.

The lines suggesting the ruts in the foreground part of the path should be horizontal . . . just a few strokes over these along the direction of the path. Then add the pebbles and stones.

Old Door—Outline and Instructions

There are seven different textures in this sketch of an old farmhouse doorway in Normandy. The wood at the top, the tiles, the brick, the light-colored stone around the door, the rough stone at the bottom, the doorway itself, and the ground.

Note that the glare effect is used in several places in this sketch—most importantly on the roof over the door. To get the full effect of the glare on the tile roof be sure that you bring the surrounding dark tone of the wood right up to the tiles. Do not leave large white areas in the cross-hatching of this surrounding wood. The sunlight also glares in a little patch of the window and alongside the door.

Put the shadow cast across the front of the building on last. Complete all the other details and hatch the shadow all at one time after putting in pencil guidelines. This will give you a more uniform shadow than if you try to put it on as you go along.

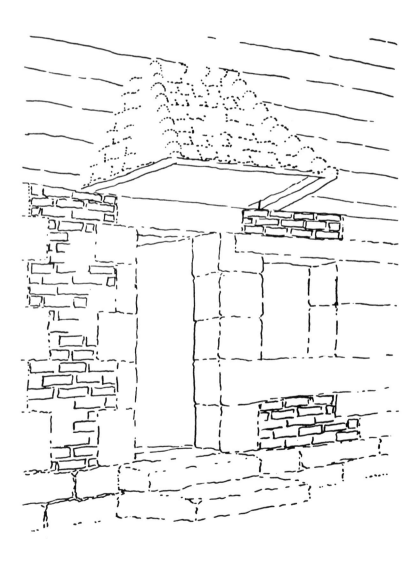

Use the flexibility of your Crowquill pen to show the shadows of the tiles as in 1 above. Then hatch some of the tiles as in 2. Leave the sun glare areas white.

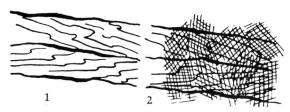

First show wood grain on the boards; then crosshatch to darken as in 2.

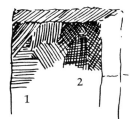 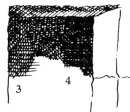

Build up the darks by crosshatching over three or four times.

Add crosshatch.

Follow these three steps to do the rough stones below the bricks. Leave the top edge of each stone white where the sun is hitting it.

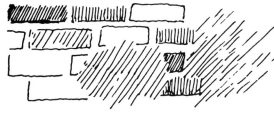

Check back to the last practice sheet and review the instructions for showing bricks before you do them in this sketch.

Stippling—Outline and Instructions

This is an introduction to stippling. It is a fascinating way to create tone and gradations of tone. You can get a subtle change and a dramatic sharp edge which are impossible to achieve with line alone.

For those of you who find stippling an interesting technique I suggest that after doing this sketch with a pen you redraw it and try it with a felt-tip pen. The felt-tip pen will make a much bigger dot, it will take much less time to complete the sketch, and you will get a very interesting coarse-grained sketch that you may even like more than the one with the pen.

More or less complete one section of this sketch at a time before you move on to the next section. It is too easy to lose important edges if you first cover too much area with the underlying initial tone.

Stippling is an especially effective way to sketch flowers when they are done on acetate or on tracing vellum and then placed over watercolor underlays.

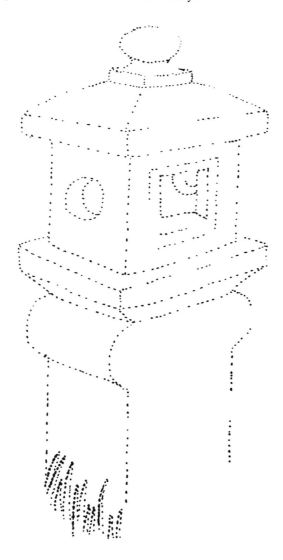

Stipple takes more time than crosshatch does but gives a quite different effect.

Take one area at a time and first put a uniform dot tone in the shaded part. Then go back and deepen where needed; define edges by additional stippling.

Only then put the texture dots sparingly in the sunny areas.

Do not put too much grass in.

Barns—Outline and Instructions

Barns are fun subjects. You will find a lot of them throughout this book. This one is a simple exercise in basically three tones—light, medium, and dark.

You have already used all the texturing techniques required for this sketch, and will simply put them together in a slightly different way here.

There are several important things here which you should not overlook. First, be certain that you indicate with pencil the little areas over the branches where they cross the dark interior of the barn. This white sliver is essential to getting the depth necessitated by the barn being behind the tree. Second, be certain to pencil some guidelines on the roof so that when you put the texture lines on it these lines will be parallel to one of the two edges that make up the roof. Unless your lines lie in one of these two directions, the shingles will tend to look like they are standing up rather than lying down.

Where dark areas come up to other features, such as the dark underneath of the barn coming to the supporting beam, be sure that you do not leave significant white patches in the darks. Go back when you are finished and trim these darks tightly to their adjacent features. This will make them distinct rather than allowing them to become a little fuzzy.

Also remember to make the shade on the grass a uniform distribution of grass marks, not patchy, checkerboard clumps with big white areas included. The shadow effect requires uniformity of tone.

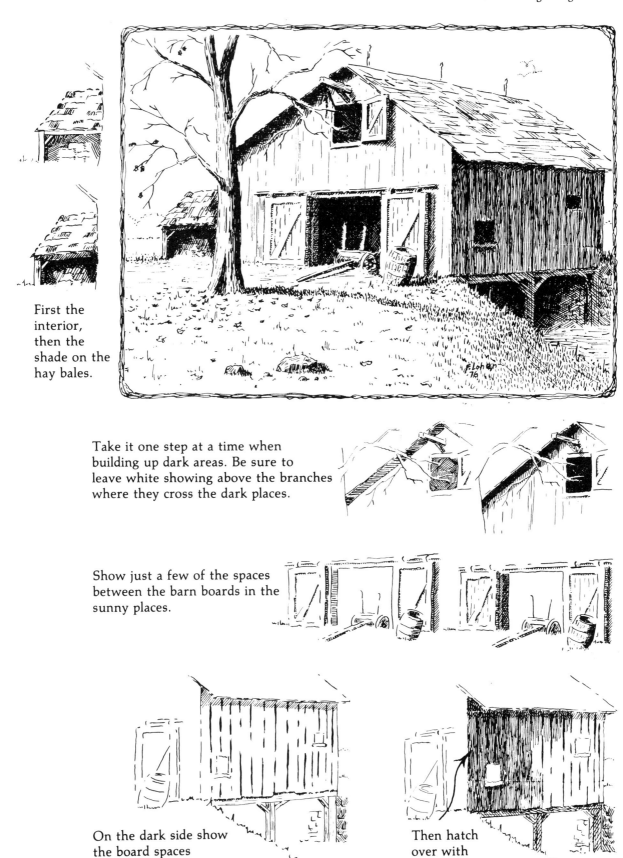

First the interior, then the shade on the hay bales.

Take it one step at a time when building up dark areas. Be sure to leave white showing above the branches where they cross the dark places.

Show just a few of the spaces between the barn boards in the sunny places.

On the dark side show the board spaces quite heavy.

Then hatch over with vertical lines only.

Castle Steps—Outline and Instructions

These castle steps (from Castle Rising in England) will require more time to sketch than any other exercise in this section of the book.

There is a lot of ink to put on the paper here. The most important thing to keep in mind when doing this sketch is the light which highlights all upper edges of stones and steps. It is this highlight, shown by a light band between dark bands on the upper set of steps, that makes them appear as steps to the viewer.

The stones in the walls all have light upper edges and dark lower edges where these surfaces catch the light and where they curve away from the light into the darkness.

Put very little line work in the brightly lit upper chamber. Remember that the brilliant sunlight is washing all detail out with its glare.

Do not lose the light front edges on the lower set of steps.

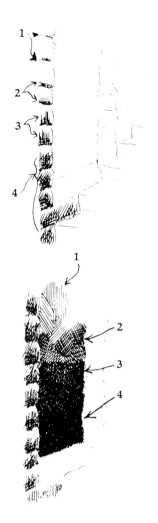

The most important thing to do in this sketch is to keep the top edges of all stones and the front edge of all steps white. The very last thing you will do is to tone them down by hatching over, only if they need it.

The bottom edges of all stones are dark.

The riser (vertical) part of each step should be darker than the tread.

Seascape—Outline and Instructions

This nautical scene is a change of pace from the preceding sketch. It does not take long to complete.

Water lies horizontal, so the strokes indicating the water should also. Do not make water too dark; use just enough strokes to establish its presence and to indicate darker reflections on its surface. Let a lot of light tell the rest of the story.

Be sure to indicate the background line of hills with your pencil before you start. Make this tone as smooth and uniform as you can—keep the lines of equal weight and spacing.

The wharf is much like the barrel in the first exercise of this section.

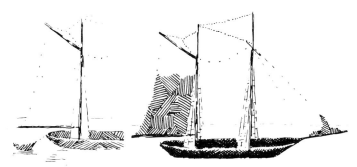

Start with the boats. Watch the white areas . . . don't lose them.

Leave some white here.

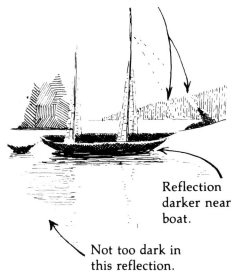

Reflection darker near boat.

Not too dark in this reflection.

Do the pilings as you did the barrel earlier.

Just a few lines in the sun.

Leave these white or they will disappear.

Hillside—Outline and Instructions

This simple little hillside scene deals primarily with the representation of the pine trees in the background and the needles on the foreground trees.

Each background tree must be constructed when represented this way. Make each of them a different height and allow more white paper to show on the sunny side of these trees than on the shadow side.

Each foliage mass of the foreground trees must also be constructed separately. Make certain that the outline of each of these masses is irregular, just the way they grow. It is very easy to make these foliage groups like round balls of cotton candy.

The shadows must follow the hillside to help create the illusion of a sloped surface. The little grass strokes also are important in this regard, so be sure to make them go uphill.

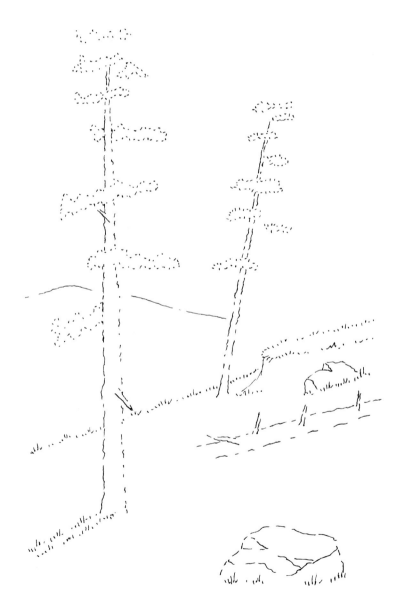

Lightly pencil in the triangular shapes for the background evergreen trees and complete them as shown.

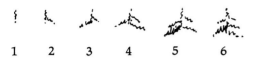

1   2   3   4   5   6

Proceed this way with the background trees.

Keep the sunny side of the background trees lighter than the shady side.

 The foreground tree foliage is made up of little clumps like this.

Do the foliage before the trunk.

 First do the darker foliage.

 Then show a little with the sun glaring on it.

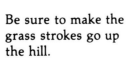 Be sure to make the grass strokes go up the hill.

Mailbox—Outline and Instructions

The last sketch in this section is a simple composition showing a rural mailbox peeking up from a mass of weeds. It is suggested that when you finish this sketch you paint the two goldenrod blossoms with yellow and orange. You will be surprised at the striking effect just a little touch of color can bring to an otherwise black-and-white sketch. Use acrylic or watercolor paints. Oils will stain the paper.

The close-up weed effect is created by showing a few weeds in full outline and then filling in between with primarily vertical grasslike strokes. Remember to keep these uniformly distributed, not bunched and patchy with lots of white in between.

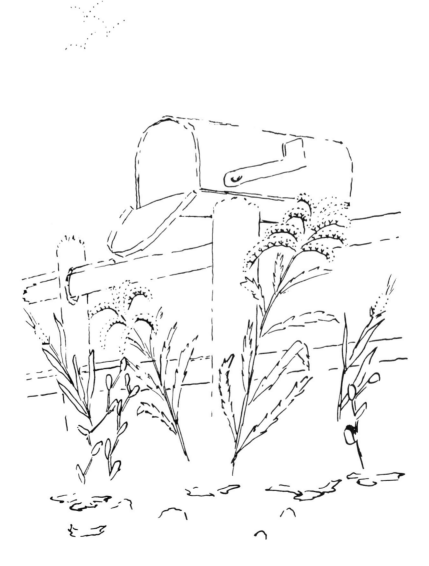

Follow the curve of the mailbox with the shading.

Then crosshatch with lines that go with the length of the mailbox.

First put some grass strokes in . . . then add some darks.

For a little different touch try painting just the two goldenrod plumes with orange and yellow.

Use watercolor or acrylic, not oil, paints.

Part III: Intermediate

There is a particular gratification the first time you have one of your sketches printed on note paper or a greeting card. It is much less expensive than most people think and is almost always received with as much satisfaction and enjoyment as it is sent. It is generally looked upon as one of the nicest personal touches you can share. A few suggestions are included at the beginning of this section that may make it easier to do this the first time.

The instructions in this section are much more general than in the beginners' section. It is assumed that through practice of the Part II subjects you have come to a point where you can look at a complete pen sketch and visualize just what steps the artist took to complete it. Having done some step-by-step examples yourself, you should be able to apply that process to new subject matter and organize your own step-by-step sequence.

One thing to remember is that in general it is best to complete the features and structural details of your sketch first and then go in and add any shading and shadows that may be required on top of the details. This will make your shades and shadows more uniform and will make any detail that shows up in them more natural looking.

For some, practice will be necessary to obtain the delicacy of touch with the pen required for such subjects as flowers and faces. For others, it will come naturally. Each one of us has an inherent, natural way of using the pen. When you have done quite a few different sketches and have practiced the work of many different artists, you will be able to bring different techniques to different subjects quite naturally, depending on how you decide a particular subject should be treated.

Sketching on the spot is quite difficult at best if you are going to include much significant detail. One sketch in this section, Near Gatlinburg, was done on the spot. The one following it was done in the studio from pencil sketches and notes made on the spot, supported by some photographs. Generally this is the way I prefer to work, as it is almost impossible to get comfortable enough in the field for a long enough period of time to complete a reasonable sized sketch. Unless you are somewhat comfortable, it is my experience that you cannot bring the concentration to your work that is required.

Greeting Cards and Notepaper

Your own creations are easy to do and inexpensive to have printed. Standard size envelopes, which can be purchased where you have the printing done, are also not very expensive.

For the standard greeting card, fold an 8½- by 11-inch sheet (standard typewriter size paper) in fourths, open it up, and do your art work and lettering as shown at C. Do not forget your *logo*, or symbol, on the back. The alternative fold is as shown at D and E.

The printing is then all on one side—you can even sign the original, and your signature will be printed also. Printing like this on 70-pound paper in black ink will cost about $6 or $7 per 100 sheets.

Colored paper and colored ink are extra. Check with your printer. You may add color with paints or with felt-tipped markers.

For note or letter paper, fold and cut a single thickness sheet to fit a standard-size envelope. Then do your art work as at F, G, or H, depending on what you want. Have it printed on 70-pound stock.

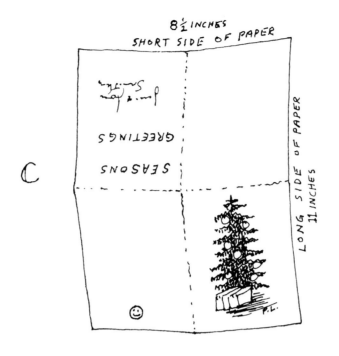

C

8½ INCHES
SHORT SIDE OF PAPER

LONG SIDE OF PAPER
11 INCHES

SEASONS GREETINGS

D

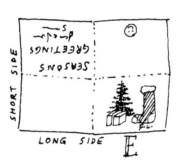

E

SHORT SIDE

LONG SIDE

SEASONS GREETINGS

F

G

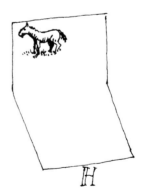

H

Background Trees

Sometimes your composition will
require background trees to be a
medium tone against which both
darker and lighter tones must be
placed. This example shows how a
uniform gray tone is first put into
the background tree area.

A very fine, Hunt No. 104, quill pen
was used for this barn and silo
sketch. The complete sketch
is on the next page.

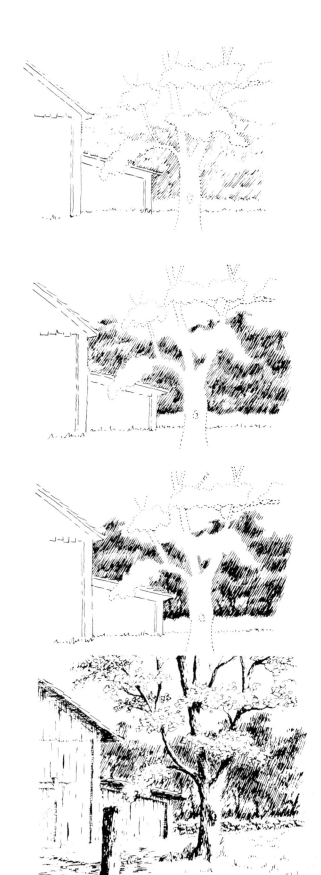

After the uniform tone is done, put
a little texture into the foliage
by going over it in patches using
strokes in the same direction as
the first ones. (The dots and lines
in these sketches represent your
pencil lines.)

Then, still using short lines and
dashes in the same direction, add
some indication of tree trunks
in the lower part of the tree
masses.

At this point you can tell just
how dark and how light the overlying
details should be to show
up well.

Note that the right side of the
big tree as well as the right
side of the barn and the shed did
not need an outline. The gray tone
behind them provided enough
definition.

Flowers

The violet and the iris were done with a Hunt No. 104 point. This is a very fine line point that the delicate markings on the petals and leaves required. The goldenrod and the daisy were done with a Crowquill.

The steps were first outlining over the pencil drawing, then indicating the major shadows, and finally just working over the leaves and petals to build up the tones to their final values.

The violet leaves have a bumpy texture that was shown by the groups of hatch marks with white spaces left between. The iris is all smooth, so lines in one direction were used.

An Old Greek Fountain

Generally, when sketching old weathered stonework follow the sequence of steps at the right side of this page. At step E the shadow at the bottom of each stone is put in and at step F some stones are darkened a little and a few are darkened a bit more by crosshatch. Note that the top edges of all the stones are left white to indicate the glare of the sun. A sketch such as the one above would be a little monotonous if all the stonework were evenly shaded, so the sunlight was allowed to wash out almost all detail toward the upper right corner.

Stone and Wrought Iron

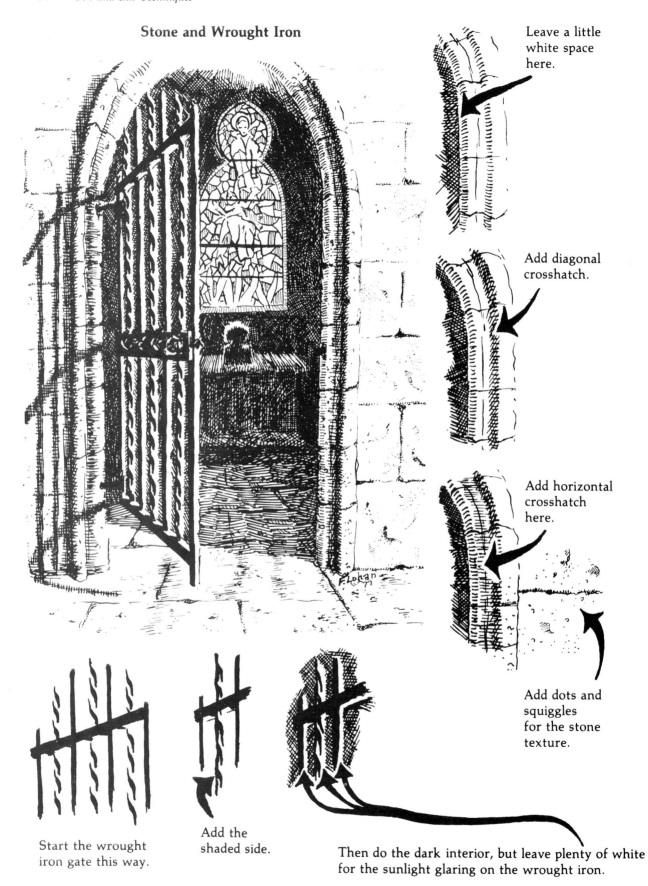

Leave a little white space here.

Add diagonal crosshatch.

Add horizontal crosshatch here.

Add dots and squiggles for the stone texture.

Start the wrought iron gate this way.

Add the shaded side.

Then do the dark interior, but leave plenty of white for the sunlight glaring on the wrought iron.

Stone Chimney

The study above of a rough stone chimney on a log cabin indicates what must be done when you are rendering highly irregular rocks.

First, in pencil, locate each rock, making sure that each is a different size and shape. Then begin to indicate the shadows from all the irregularities on each stone surface.

As you add the gray tone and darken the shadows, be sure to leave a few highlights on the stones. The mortar between the stones was done with stipple marks to get a texture that contrasts with the stones.

Finish up by final darkening the shadows and adding shadow on the material between the stones. Finally make a few of the stones darker than the others.

Outlines were not necessary on the left-hand edge of the chimney stones, because they were left in the highlight with a darker tone behind.

Animals

These, like any other sketches, begin with a good pencil outline drawing that shows all features and also locates all dark markings and major shadow areas.

Furry or feathery edges are then shown in a furry or feathery manner with ink by broken lines and dots and short lines in the direction of the fur or feathers. Very little solid outline should be used.

The eyes should be put in, but do not make them too dark at first. When the entire animal sketch is about complete, you go over it to bring the darks to their appropriate final value.

Now the dark markings are blocked in, again not to what you think their final value should be. The shadowed areas are also blocked in.

The three subjects above are shown at this stage; the lighter fur and feather work is not yet being started. As you do start the lighter indications, you darken the dark areas as you go so that the kind of contrast necessary is developed. The chipmunk's head is shown at this stage.

The next page shows these three sketches brought to completion, along with three additional subjects.

This horse sketch follows the same steps just discussed for animals.

First a good pencil outline is required, followed by hatching in the major dark areas and shadows. This step is shown above.

Then the medium tone is applied, at the same time building up the dark areas as they need it. This step frequently requires going over several times to get the proper contrasts rather than going for the darkest darks the first time. You can see from the completed sketch at the right that, in this case, the strokes did not all follow the direction of the hair on the animal.

For a subject of this kind a good photograph is essential. You must get the proper shape and proportions as well as the pattern of skin folds on the animals.

The eyes and skin folds are done first as above. Then the shading is crosshatched, as at the right. As you do the shading, darken the skin folds where they need it so as not to lose them except in the darkest shadow areas.

Be sure to minimize or eliminate the details in the highlighted areas and to build up the very dark parts gradually.

Near Gatlinburg, Tennessee

This was a quick sketch, about an hour, done on the spot. Start with an outline of each rock and the tree.

Build up the shading and form on each rock. Take them one at a time, using the direction of the hatch lines to indicate the slope of each rock surface.

Then put the water in, using your darkest tones close to the rocks. Keep all water strokes horizontal. Use very few strokes in the flowing water where it is white. Next do the background trees and finally complete the foreground tree and add the darkest trees in the background.

In the Great Smoky Mountains

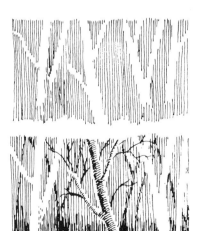

This scene is similar to the preceding one but, being larger, it required more detailed attention to the background treatment. As shown at the left, the background starts with a uniform tone that skips the larger background trees. These areas were first penciled in as a guide for inking.

Then the shrubbery was darkened, the closer of the background trees were toned and their branches added, and the darker background trees were put in over the gray tone. These additions are shown at the left.

This was done in the studio from a pencil sketch made on location. Note that very few outlines were used on the rocks. Compare with preceding page.

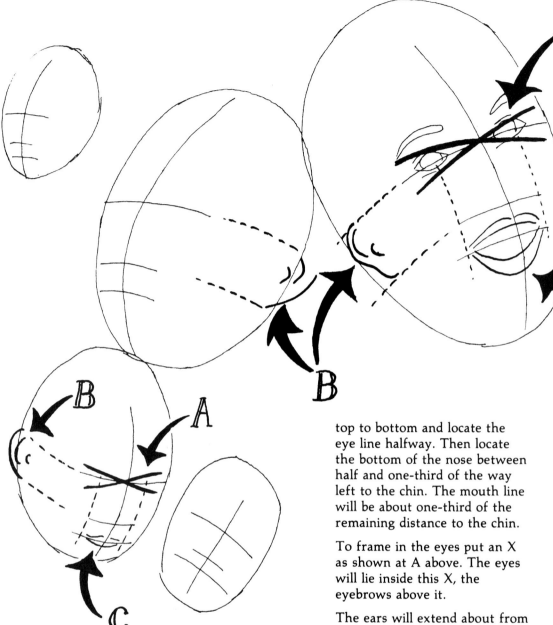

Faces

Sketching faces is not easy. Any lack of symmetry becomes very obvious. The following procedure will help you to produce a reasonably good sketch.

Start with an egg-shaped outline for the head. The eyes are located approximately halfway down on the head. Draw a center line for the face from top to bottom and locate the eye line halfway. Then locate the bottom of the nose between half and one-third of the way left to the chin. The mouth line will be about one-third of the remaining distance to the chin.

To frame in the eyes put an X as shown at A above. The eyes will lie inside this X, the eyebrows above it.

The ears will extend about from the eye line to the nose line for women, for men from the eye line about to the mouth line. This is shown at B above for women's faces.

The mouth is about as wide as the center distance of the eyes, as shown at C above.

Everyone's face is a little different—remember, these are approximate proportions.

Now you start on the features.

Using the egg-shaped outline as a guide, finalize the facial contour, eye, nose, mouth, and hairline details. Add the neck and shoulder lines as well as lines indicating skin folds, such as above and below the eyes and in the neck. Smiling faces generally also show lines from the nose toward the corners of the mouth.

By now your sketch will be full of lines and erasures but should be properly proportioned. Then trace or transfer only the final facial lines and details to your working sheet of paper in pencil.

Add circles for the highlight on the eyes and begin to indicate the features with ink.

Using the pencil lines from the last step as a guide, crosshatch the eyebrows and the dark parts of the eyes. *Do not make these features too dark at this point:* they will be touched up near the completion of your sketch. Only then can you determine whether or not they need to be darker.

Use lines sparingly. A row of hatch marks does the best job of showing the soft facial shadows and many of the lines that appear in the face.

Add the major shadow areas of the face, first outlining these areas with a pencil. Put in the hair. If it is dark hair crosshatch will do; if it is light hair just use lines that flow in the direction of the hair.

Then go over the whole sketch to darken where necessary and touch up where it seems to need it.

This pretty woman is shown along with six of her pretty friends on the next page.

Be careful with lines on the face. A few too many can age a young face.

When showing teeth *do not draw the spaces between the teeth.*

Scratchboard

Simulating Woodcuts

Scratchboard is a heavy paper coated with a thin clay layer. You can paint india ink on the scratchboard with a brush and, when it is dry, scratch through the ink with a sharp tool to get white lines. This is shown at A and B above.

To simulate a woodcut, as at the top of the page, do your drawing on a separate sheet and transfer it to the scratchboard by rubbing a pencil on the back of the drawing and tracing it onto the scratchboard. Then, with a small brush or a round-point pen, outline the entire sketch in ink. The ink for technical or artist's fountain pens is best for scratchboard work. Paint in the dark areas and draw the background lines as at C.

With a sharp tool, scratch the white spaces from the lines you drew for the background into the painted black ink as at D. Also scratch the white above the ropes. Then, with your round-point pen, put in the details of the subject (a sharp-pointed pen will dig into the clay surface). You can easily trim lines and create white areas, such as the light clouds in the sketch at the top of the page, by scratching the ink away. You can also go over the scratched area with ink.

Portraits

This page shows another use for scratchboard. The drawing was transferred to the board in pencil. The pencil lines are shown as dots at the right. Waterproof technical-pen india ink was then painted over the dark areas as at the right.

Then the tones were put in with a technical pen (Rapidograph type), starting as shown with the top of the beret. You must work lightly with the pen so as not to scratch into the surface of the board.

The sketch below shows how far the tone work was carried before the scratchboard tool was used. This subject was sketched from an 8 by 10 color photograph that showed all facial details very clearly.

CAUTION! When using scratchboard by sure you make your pencil drawing on the correct side. Both sides look and feel the same, although only one side is coated. Make a little scratch at one corner of the sheet and you can tell if it is the correct side.

The scratchboard tool was then used to soften the edges of the dark areas and to put highlights on the eyes and above and below the dark-side eye and highlights on the beret and on the neck. The moustache and hair were also scratched in. Alternate with scratching and using the pen until it all looks right to you.

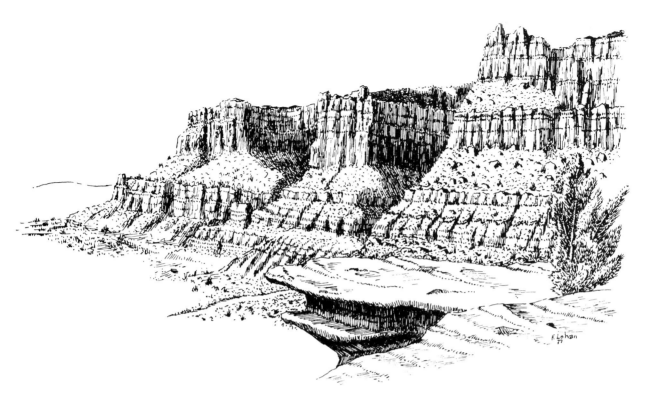

A Utah Panorama

A scene like this can seem overwhelmingly complicated but really is not. The keys are the horizontal strata lines and the shadows in the eroded vertical faces of the cliffs.

The first step is a pencil drawing as below, showing the outline of the formations and the horizontal lines representing the darker layers of rock and the cliff faces. For the moment ignore all other detail in your pencil sketch, as it would tend to confuse things.

The second step is to put in the dark, narrow horizontal layers. Use rows of vertical ines and dots for this indication as shown in the sketch below.

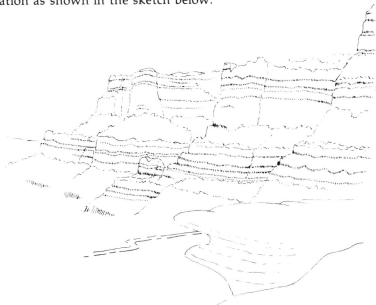

Then, taking one section of the sketch at a time and using vertical lines only, darken the shadowed areas and put a few vertical lines in the sunlit places. Do not put too much in the sunny spots or you will lose the contrast with the darks. Keep the bundles of lines vertical on the cliff faces and let the bundles slope on the eroded lower slopes. This establishes your contours. The sketch below is at this stage.

Then, with dots, squiggles, and hatch marks, complete the remaining parts of the sketch.

Working from Photographs

The subject above was taken from a photograph of Capitol Reef, Utah. All you can get from a photo for pen and ink sketching is a composition. At least 90 percent or more of the detail in a photo must be ignored for a pen sketch. You can only indicate the very essence of the subject—in the case above it was the horizontal strata and the vertical cliffs. It takes a lot of practice and many failures to know what must be ignored in the photo and what must be emphasized to capture the idea of the subject. This should not discourage you but should simply make you aware that it takes a lot of practice before you will get consistently good results.

An Old Cedar Tree

Starting with a pencil outline, show the dark cracks in the trunk and branches. Then go over these areas with lines that flow with the wood grain, building up the darker tones by piling more lines on top but in the same direction. When all the wooden parts are finished, put in the foliage, grass, and rock. Notice that there was no crosshatch used in this sketch. The last step is to put in the shadows cast on the trunk by some of the branches.

Part IV: Reference

This section of the book is meant to be a source of ideas for you when you are sketching on your own. Of course it can serve as a source of practice ideas for you, as can any good line work you find in books, magazines, and newspapers. But primarily I tried here to include a wide variety of material that would serve to get you going when you reach that point at which you know what you want to sketch but do not know just how to start. In this section you may find some similar element and, from my rendition of it, get at least one idea as to how to execute it in your own sketch. As I have stated before, there is no *one* right way to sketch anything. If you try for an effect and are not satisfied with it, try a different way.

Frequently, when I am undecided as to just how to render a detail, I put a sheet of tracing vellum over the sketch and try several things. In this way one can get a good idea of how the approach will look without risking the final sketch.

No one book can be exhaustive on a subject as wide and varied as this. At best, a book can only whet the appetite with a few hors d'oeuvres and perhaps point the way to other substantial sustenance. For you, your interest in this medium will make you aware of line work in many places it has always existed but has eluded your eye. To build on the hors d'oeuvres in this book, make a habit of collecting examples of pen work. You can accumulate a wealth of reference material by clipping things from magazines and newspapers when they catch your eye. These should be studied and even copied in part to learn how certain effects were achieved. Keep in mind, however, that many line-type effects are produced photographically these days. Such illustrations are very effective and can serve as excellent technique sources, but do not expect to accomplish exactly what the camera did. It can be a lot of fun trying, however.

A Practice Sketchbook

It is a good idea to keep your little practice sketches in a notebook of some kind. You will frequently want to re-sketch some of them, changing the composition, trying other details, changing the lighting or the textures.

You can make your sketches on any kind of paper, put a freehand border on them, cut them out, and put them in your notebook with rubber cement.

The center sketch on this page was done in at least a dozen different ways and different sizes over a two-year period. Some of these were watercolors, some were pen and ink, and one was acrylic. All were different in certain respects but were of the same basic scene.

Compare the sketch at the bottom of the page on clapboard siding later in this book with the center sketch on this page to see what I mean.

Practice Sketchbook Ideas

A Hunt No. 104 pen point was used to sketch most of the smaller sketches in this book.

Many of these sketches were done on the backs of index cards, which offer a stiff, smooth surface that takes ink well.

Paper is quite abrasive and will wear out a fine point after 20 or 30 sketches of this size. Get a new point when you notice that you can no longer make the very fine lines that small sketches require. Keep the old point for larger sketches.

Quick Sketches for Practice

Until you have sketched quite a bit, it is difficult to "invent" a practice scene. Look at magazines, calendars, the newspaper for an idea you can simplify into a quick sketch to get the practice you need so that you will be ready for that important sketch you will want to frame. These practice sketches do not have to be masterpieces. They are simply opportunities to try various things with the pen.

Any paper that takes ink well will do for practice. The backs of index cards are good; bond paper is also good. Bristol board pads are very good for your "masterpieces."

Foregrounds

Foregrounds should never compete for attention with the main subject. However, there should be something interesting in every part of your sketch, something that helps to establish the setting.

In the two sketches at the top of this page, notice how the one on the right looks more complete than the one on the left. The totally interest-devoid foreground on the left just doesn't feel right.

The foreground interest can be a stone, a tree, a curb, or simply the shadow from a structure that is not in the sketch.

In the bottom, left, sketch, the dark-against-light/light-against-dark principle was used in the foliage of the foreground tree and its placement in front of the barn.

Trees

Isolated trees make charming focal points for simple landscape sketches. The pen strokes should indicate the nature of the foliage, but the shape, placement, and shading of the leaf masses count more for overall effectiveness than the particular way in which the foliage is drawn.

Note the many different ways that foliage is drawn in the sketches in this book and practice them all. Look for sketches by other artists and practice them, also. Only then can you decide what your technique should be.

First put leaf masses in; then ink the tree.

More Trees

Each species of tree has a different characteristic outline and foliage grouping. Do not always put the same tree in your landscape sketches.

Practice all different kinds of trees—from these sketches, from photographs and, best of all, directly from nature.

Draw your tree in pencil, indicate the masses of leaves (some on the near side of the tree covering the trunk, some on the far side darker, with the trunk showing), ink the leaf masses, and then ink in the trunk. Don't forget the shadow under the tree.

Foreground Trees

Trees in the foreground require more detailed modeling and shading. If branches cross over the trunk, be sure to leave a white, un-inked space over or alongside them or they will disappear.

Foliage on foreground trees requires more detail, also. Draw your branches in pencil, then ink the leaves on the branches, then ink the branches. Show enough leaves but not too many.

An old scar from a missing branch is often appropriate, also.

If the tree is the focal point, keep the background extremely simple.

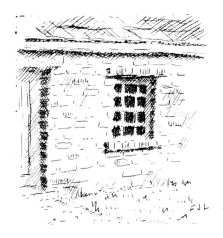

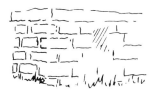

First outline the bricks you want to show.

Then darken those in the shade and a few in the sun.

Then finish the shading and the shadows.

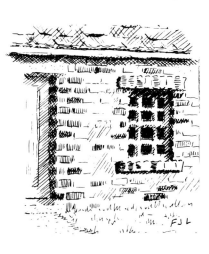

Bricks

There are usually four distinct tones when showing brickwork. First, some bricks are missing . . . not shown at all, just some hatching over that area. Second, some bricks are just drawn in outline or in partial outline, showing only the two shaded sides. Third, most bricks are shown with a medium tone by hatching. Fourth, a few are shown dark by crosshatching or darker hatching.

Draw the brick courses in pencil first so the bricks will lie in straight rows. The direction of lines that tone the bricks does not matter; they can be vertical, horizontal, or at any angle.

In shadow, more of the bricks are shown darker; then the whole shaded area, bricks and all, is hatched over.

Brickwork

This architectural drawing shows a treatment of bricks in a wall. Note that horizontal, vertical, and lines at an angle were used to show individual bricks. The wall in shade was hatched over entirely.

Take note of the simplified treatment of the background trees.

Stonework

As with the bricks, there are four distinct tones in stonework. But the stones are not lined up and are not all the same size.

Sometimes a dark mortar is used between the stones, so the joint lines must be shown dark as in the upper right sketch.

In the sketch below, note how the dots indicating the shadow from the window mullion strips on the curtains enhance the illusion of depth.

Barns

As with anything else, in close-up sketching more detail is required than when the subject is in the middle ground or background. When farther back, the only prominent thing is the darker spaces between the boards. When in the foreground, some indications of the wood grain and rough surface are required.

Barns are always interesting sketch subjects and can be quickly done for practice.

Different Techniques

There is no one *correct* way to sketch anything. Here the same scene is shown in two different ways. One is no more valid than the other. Copy the work of different artists so that you will come to see how they achieved their particular effects and at the same time give yourself more practice.

When you show puddles, be sure that something quite contrasty reflects in them. The edges of puddles are dark because of the wet mud, but where the water touches the mud it curves up and reflects the sky. That is why the thin white line shows between water and mud.

Drawn at
larger scale.

Shingle Siding

Shingle siding is characteristic of buildings in many parts of the country. It is distinguished by the shadow from the bottom of the overlapping pieces. A few of the vertical spaces between the shingles are also shown. They are generally darkened, some darker than the others except where the glare of the sun striking them removes almost all visible detail.

Use pencil guidelines to keep the shingles relatively even, although you want a little irregularity from shingle to shingle.

Clapboard Siding

As with the shingle siding, the thing that distinguishes clapboard is the shadow from the bottoms of the overlapping boards. These shadows can be shown with horizontal lines or with rows of dots, as illustrated above. Remember to use pencil lines first so they come out straight.

Glare is used on the roof and on the front of the main building below to create contrast at the center of interest.

Where wires (or ropes or twigs and branches) cross dark areas, leave white paper showing above them as in the sketch below.

Stucco

Stucco is generally light-colored with a fine, granular texture. It is best shown by stippling when it is close-up, but with just enough stippling, not all over the surface. It is frequently cracked, also, and sometimes the underlying bricks show through where it has cracked off.

Old post-and-beam buildings were often stuccoed between the beams.

If the subject is too far away to use stippling for indicating the stucco, just show the surface with an even tone—white in the sunlight and lightly but evenly hatched in the shade.

The Old Bookstore

The sketch above illustrates many of the things just stated about sketching wood and stucco in a foreground subject. The stippling is like pepper on food—too much spoils it. Note how stippling was also used to indicate the smooth stonework on the building to the left of the subject.

Take note how the glare of sunlight is used to break up the relative monotony of the slate roof and of all the little glass panes in the storefront.

Rocks

In shoreline sketches rocks often play an important part—more so than the occasional rock that lends interest to a landscape sketch.

Rocks should not look like potatoes piled up. They have flat surfaces and cracks and planes intersecting at different angles.

The planes are shown by lines and sometimes dots, and the surfaces of these planes are then defined by hatching lines.

1 Indicate planes of the rock in outline.

2 Then indicate planes with a few lines and shadows.

Rocky Shoreline

When rocks are in the foreground, more detail is required than when they are in the background. In this sketch rocks stretch all the way from the very foreground into the distance.

You can see that the rocks in the distance are nothing more than outlines, with the upper surfaces left white and the sides shaded. Those in the foreground show many planes and deeper shadows than those in the background.

Boats

Boats are most often of wood and hence are sketched as wood. Try to minimize outlining and rather let the intersection of a highlighted surface with a surface that is toned define an edge. The front of the boat at the left shows what is meant.

Note too how the rope is left whitest where it crosses the shadowed side of the boat. This contrast creates interest.

The rocks in the foreground below do not show great contrast. They are there only to help establish the setting, not to compete with the boat.

More Boats

As stated earlier, there is no one *right* way to sketch anything. This page shows the same boat textured in two different ways. Although outlining has been kept to an absolute minimum in both sketches, the same subject could be rendered in outline only or in solid blacks and whites.

Ships

Even as derelicts there is something stately about fully rigged ships and their masts and lines and spars and chains.

Curved surfaces such as hulls require a gradual transition from dark tone to white glare in order to capture the *idea* of a curved surface.

In any water scenes reflections are important. In this sketch the water is shown in between glassy calm and rough, and the reflections are quite indistinct.

Seaside Scenes

These three sketches show the importance of contrast between light and dark. In the top sketch the sails are shown dark against a light sky. That and all the marvelous clutter of the rigging pulls the eye to that ship.

In the middle sketch the background trees were made dark to frame in the fishhouse. The little white boat and its white reflection pop right out against the dark ship.

In the bottom sketch the water is very calm and the reflections are more mirror-like. The alternating light and dark pattern of the pilings makes them prominent—and required care not to make them too uniform.

Snow Scenes

When showing evergreen trees in a snow scene, leave more white showing on the sunny sides than you would in a sketch showing another season.

Snow scenes allow nice contrasts between dark and light. To establish a snow scene, however, requires something to put snow on, such as roofs of barns or houses. That, and the lack of grass strokes in the white areas, says *snow*.

A few weeds should pop through and perhaps bushes and trees with no foliage (or corn stalks, as in the bottom sketch).

Fur and Feathers

Sketching fur and feathers realistically comes only with practice. The darker markings on the owl were put in first, and then hatching and cross-hatching were built up over them until the desired effect was achieved.

A Hunt No. 104 pen point was used for all the hatching on the owl and for the fine markings on the tree. A Crowquill (Hunt No. 102) was used for the rest of the sketch.

Outline Sketches

When using outline and little or no tone in a sketch, keep the lines loose and free and not continuous.

A good pencil outline is usually essential, so that you get the correct shape and proportion before you start to ink the sketch.

Compare the upper right sketch on this page with the same subject, done larger using a watercolor brush, later in this book.

Note that there is no more detail in the larger sketch than in the smaller.

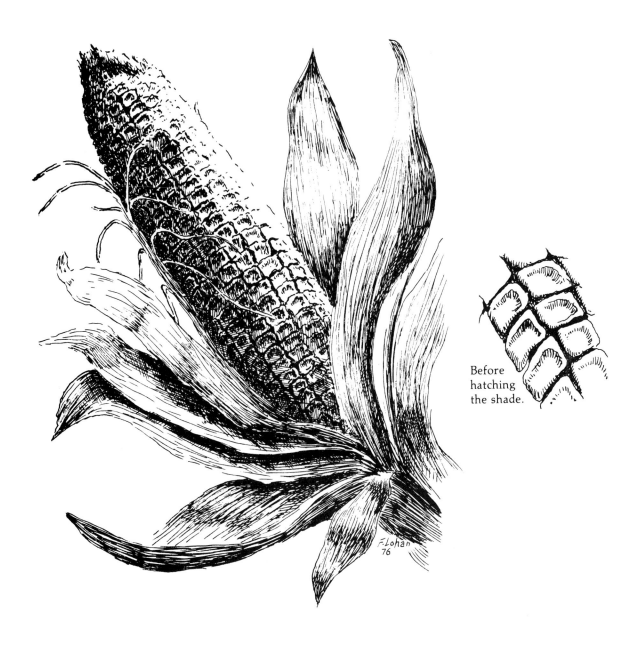

Before
hatching
the shade.

Ear of Corn

This sketch was started with a detailed pencil drawing outlining each kernel of dried corn. The dark spaces between the kernels were then inked, followed by the "dimples" in each kernel. Then the whole cob was hatched and crosshatched to get the desired shading. The leaves were done last, gradually building up the darks until they were right. A final touch-up to darken some of the spaces between the kernels completed the sketch.

Close-up Faces

Faces are not easy. They are less easy when done close-up. Basically, the tone lines should follow the contours of the face, with deeper tones next to highlights doing the modeling of the features. Outlining would spoil a sketch such as this one.

Fountain Pen Sketches

Many times, especially when traveling, it is convenient to use an ordinary fountain pen to make sketches. These generally have a very firm point that allows no flexibility in line width. This lack of flexibility forces a freer, more direct approach to the sketch, with less attention being given to detail. The sketch therefore can be done quickly and be fun to do.

Be careful, however, as moisture from your hand can smear the lines.

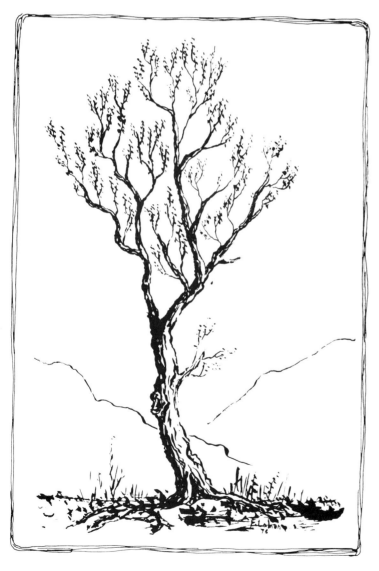

Brush Sketches

These sketches were done with a No. 000 watercolor brush and india ink.

There is less control of the brush, which gives a freer sketch. Yet fine, pen-like lines can be made.

You will find the brush faster than the pen, and you may even find it more fun to use.

Even with the brush, it is still a good idea to make a pencil sketch on which to put the ink.

Dried ink will ruin a watercolor brush. Be sure to wash it out with warm water and soap when you complete a sketch.

A Brush and Ink Portrait

This action portrait was done with a No. 2 watercolor brush and india ink. It was based on the little pen sketch of the same subject shown as an outline sketch on page 86.

The wash technique can also be used with india ink and brush. First put in the darks and outlines you want with undiluted india ink. Then show the tones with ink diluted to various degrees with water. Be sure to use the waterproof india ink for washes.

Drawing with Twigs and Other Things

The sketch to the left was done using a little dried twig dipped in india ink. The more flexible the twig and the farther back you hold it, the looser your sketch will be.

This can be a relaxing change of pace after completing a tight little pen sketch.

The sketch at the right was done using a small palette knife dipped into india ink and then dragged across the paper. At the bottom a cloth piece was folded and dipped into the ink and then was pressed on the paper to get the dotted tone behind the dark grass blades.

Your imagination is the only limitation to creativity and enjoyment with pen and ink sketching. It is, next to pencil sketching, the simplest, least messy visual art form to do.

Good luck!

Bibliography

Borgman, Harry. *Drawing in Ink.* New York: Watson-Guptill Publications, 1977.

Guptill, Arthur L. *Rendering in Pen and Ink.* New York: Watson-Guptill Publications, 1976. *Note:* The out-of-print, earlier versions of this work, published in the 1920s, are much more comprehensive. They remain the definitive works on the subject and are worth looking for in libraries and in secondhand shops.

Lohan, Frank. *Pen and Ink Themes.* Chicago: Contemporary Books, Inc., 1981.

Pitz, Henry C. *Ink Drawing Techniques.* New York: Watson-Guptill Publications, 1957.